ANGER MANAGEMENT
SKILLS FOR CHILDREN

MIDDLE SCHOOL

IDA GREENE, Ph.D.

ISBN 1-881165-24-8

ATTENTION COLLEGES AND UNIVERSITIES, CORPORATIONS, AND PROFESSIONAL ORGANIZATIONS: Quantity discounts are available on bulk purchases of this book for educational training purposes, fund raising, or gift giving. For information contact: **P. S. I. Publishers, 2910 Baily Ave. San Diego, CA 92105 (619) 262-9951.**

FOREWORD

We are feeling, caring, and reacting persons, which is good. The problem is that we sometimes overreact, react at the wrong time, or react in a manner that hurts others.

Hopefully, this workbook will be a useful tool to help you respond appropriately to others; so that your verbal communication, physical communication (body language) and your emotional communication is experienced in a pleasant manner.

All emotions are good, your interactions and communication patterns will determine how people will think about you, feel about you, or how they will respond to you.

ACKNOWLEDGEMENTS

I give thanks for both the good and unpleasant encounters I have experienced. I give thanks for the pleasant and unpleasant people I have met, I have learned from both.

Some life lessons can be taught and other lessons have to be bought through your trial and error, pain and hardship.

Hopefully you will be a student of life and learn from the mistakes of others.

I wish to thank Catherine Bozigian for creating the charts in this book.

Ida Greene, Ph.D.

ANGER MANAGEMENT SKILLS FOR MIDDLE SCHOOL

Definition of Anger

Everybody has his or her own definition of anger. Webster's New World Dictionary defines it as a noun, "*a feeling of displeasure, resulting from injury, mistreatment, opposition, which shows itself in a desire to fight back at the supposed cause that created the feeling.*"

We define anger as:

- An emotion that is physically arousing with unique results.
- A physiological (bodily) movement.
- A feeling that has an effect on the way you experience your world.
- A communicator of feelings, anger sends information to others.
- A cause, anger produces specific effects and results.

THINK ABOUT YOUR DEFINITION OF ANGER

Write your thoughts below:
Descriptive words to understand me better are:

1. ....

2. ....

3. ....

4. ....

....

....

....

Effective communication puts the burden on you, the sender, to insure there is understanding of the meaning of your intended message to the other person. Do not others to read your mind and try to figure out what you intend to say? Do you follow up on faulty or misunderstood communication, do you assume the worst, or leave it to the other person to figure what you meant to say?

Write your answer below.

....
....
....
....
....
....
....
....
....
....
....

STRENGTHENING MY CHARACTER

ANSWER THE QUESTIONS BELOW.

1. What are your best qualities? ....
    ....

2. What talents do you have that other children/students don't have? ....
    ....

3. What talent/skills would you like, but don't have right now?
    ....

4. What qualities do you like the most in adults?..............
    ....

5. What qualities do you like the least in adults? ....
    ....

6. What qualities do you have that you want to change?
    ....

7. Would you like help or advice to change a behavior or attitude? (Check one)

    Yes ☐   **No** ☐

TRUST ME!

ANSWER THE QUESTIONS BELOW:

Five people I trust are

- ....
- ....
- ....
- ....
- ....

I trust them because ....

....

....

....

I think ....*(number)* people trust me.

They trust me because ....

....

....

....

I can earn other people's trust by ....

....

....

....

MY PERFECT FAMILY

If you could change your family, what would it look like? Draw yourself at the larger circle, and the rest of your ideal family in the other circles. Then on the lines below, write why you would like each person to be in your family.

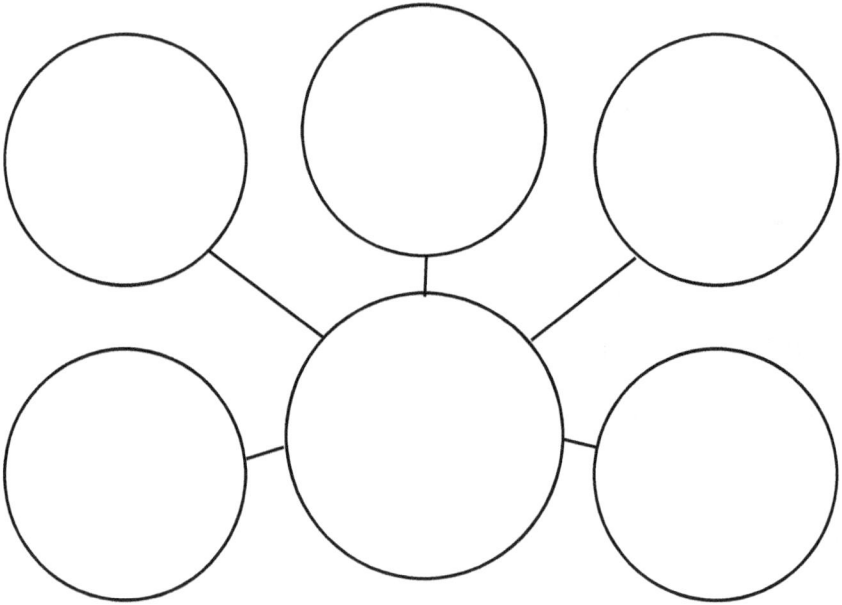

....

....

....

....

....

MY REAL FAMILY

In the spaces below, write the the names of five members of your family. Across from their name, tell what you like to do with that person.

FAMILY MEMBER
Example: Mom

WHAT I LIKE TO DO WITH THEM
Example: Play games, dance

1. _____

1. _____

_____

2. _____

2. _____

_____

3. _____

3. _____

_____

4. _____

4. _____

_____

5. _____

5. _____

_____

If I Could Change My Appearance

Some people aren't happy with the way they look and want to change a few things about themselves. Maybe you don't like the way your body looks or the size of your feet. Draw what you look like now in one box and in the other; draw what you want to look like.

ME NOW   HOW I WANT TO BE

You Can Count On Me!

We all count upon others for certain things. How do you count on these people and what do they count on you for? Complete the blanks below.

I count on Mom or Dad for	I count on my teacher for
_____ _____	_____ _____ .
My Mom or Dad counts on me to	My teacher counts on me to
_____ _____	_____ _____
I count on my friend for	I count on my brother or sister for
_____ _____	_____ _____
My friend counts on me for	He or she counts on me to
_____ _____	_____ _____

Story Time

Write a short story including all of the characters below. Talk about what they do together, if they get along, and what they might fight about.

Dr. Blue   **Mr. Smiles**   **Miss Grumpy**   **Sir Yells a Lot**

Example: Mr. Smiles doesn't like to play with Miss Grumpy a lot because she isn't as happy as he is.

....

....

....

....

....

....

....

....

....

....

....

....

WHAT I WANTED

Everyone has wanted something special. Maybe you wanted a dog or a new game. Sometimes, when we don't get these things, we feel bad. Answer the questions below about what you felt like when you didn't get what you wanted.

The special thing I wanted was:	I wanted it because:.............. ....
What did you want it for? (Birthday, holidays, etc.)	Who did you want to do it? ....
Why didn't you get it?	Were you mad? ....

The next time I don't get what I want, instead of feeling mad, I'm going to:

....

....

....

....

DRAW IT!

Choose two people you know – they could be family members, friends or even teachers. Draw one picture of what they look like when they're happy and another of when they're mad. Then circle which picture of each person that you like better.

Happy   Mad

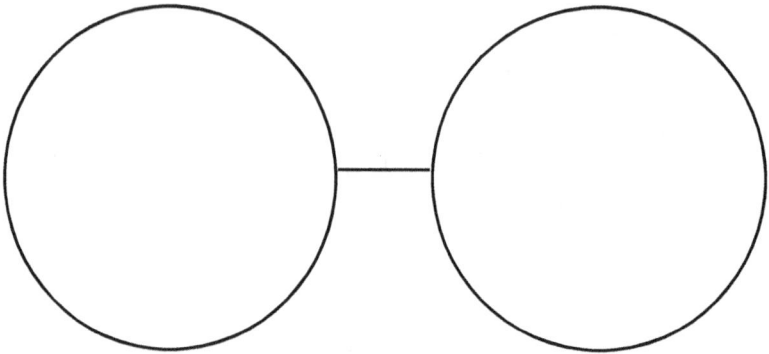

Happy   Mad

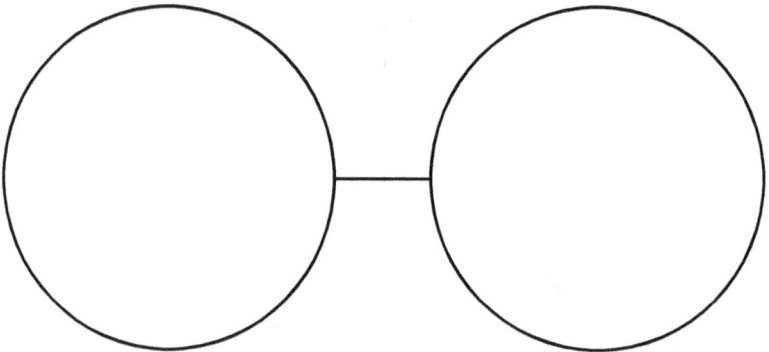

NECESSARY RULES

Answer the questions below:

1. What would your house be like if you didn't have rules?

   ....

   ....

   ....

2. What would school be like if we didn't have rules?

   ....

   ....

   ....

3. If you were the teacher, what rules would you make for the class? List the three most important rules.

   a. ....

   b. ....

   c. ....

4. Would you make rules against hurting people's feelings? What would be some good rules?

   ....

   ....

   ....

5. What would be the punishment for breaking the rules?

   ....

   ....

   ....

My New Rules

Answer the questions below:

1. What rules should be set for younger brothers and sisters to follow?...
   ....
   ....

2. What rules should be set for older brothers and sisters to follow? ....
   ....

3. What new rules would you make for your family?
   ....
   ....

4. What new rules would you set for your school?
   ....
   ....

5. What new rules would you set for children and adults to follow? ....
   ....
   ....

6. If children and adults followed the same rules, what would it be like? ....
   ....
   ....

14

The Classroom

Answer the questions below:

1. In which ways is the classroom like a family?

   ....

   ....

   ....

2. What type of members of the family is there? Who is the parent?

   ....

   ....

   ....

3. List how a school is like a society.

   ....

   ....

   ....

4. If you were the ruler of the class, would it be very controlled (dictatorship), democracy, (freedom to express oneself), or a monarchy (King or President)?

   ....

   ....

   ....

   ....

Some Interesting Things About Me

Complete the following sentences:

1. My favorite subjects in school are ....

   ....

2. My best subject is ....

   I need to improve ....

3. I like to work *By Myself**With Others* (*circle one*)

4. *I like*\|*I don't like* to read books (*circle one*)

5. *I do*\|I *don't* go to the library (*circle one*)

6. One of the best book, I ever read was ....

   ....

8. I read .... books a month.

9. At recess I like to ....

   ....

10. In physical education I like to play ....

    ....

11. After school I like to ....

    ....

12. On weekends I ....

    ....

13. My chores at home are ....

    ....

14. On TV I like to watch ....

....

15. I feel good when ....

....

16. My Hobbies are ....

....

17 I feel angry when ....

....

18. My favorite game is ....

19. When I grow up, I would like to be ....

....

20. *I do* | *I don't* have a pet.(*circle one*) it is a ....

....

21. I have traveled to ....

22. If I could travel anywhere in the world, I would go to ..

....

TEN YEARS FROM NOW

As people get older, a lot of things change about them. They may have a different hair color or a different job.

Pretend that you are ten years older and imagine what life would be like. Draw a picture of what you think you would look like in ten years and also write about how your ideas may have changed since you were in school.

....

....

....

....

....

....

....

....

Discourtesy is the beginnings of violence.

WHAT MAKES ME MAD

Answer the questions below:

Five people I get mad at are

_____,

_____,

_____,

_____ and

_____

I get mad at them because ....

....

....

....

I think people get mad at me in the same way.

They get mad at me because ....

....

....

....

I can stop making people mad by ....

....

....

....

THINK ABOUT YOUR FEELINGS OF ANGER

Are you a considerate person?
Do you feel you should get away at the expense of others?

Write your thoughts below:

....

....

....

....

....

....

Do you expect others to read your mind and try to figure out what you intend to say?
Do you follow up when there is misunderstanding in your communication or do you assume the worst?

Write your response below:

....

....

....

....

....

....

....

....

....

....

....

ANGER MANAGEMENT – BASIC CONCEPTS

To Change Your Expression of Anger, You Must Change Your Thinking

RETHINK
Change what you say to yourself in your head, in response to the external event.

1. Anger is a powerful emotion.
2. Reason is not employed when we are angry.
3. Anger is the results of jumping to conclusions about an outcome.
4. Anger creates a sense of energy, excitement and negative aliveness
5. Anger is self-serving
6. Anger is addictive/obsessive thinking you can't let go.
7. Anger is about power and control
8. Anger is used to scare, instill fear in others and as an outlet to get rid of the negative inner feelings you do not know how to handle.
9. You do not have the right to hurt another person with your anger.
10. No one has given you permission to hurt them because of your inability to handle your problems.
11. When you are angry, you are out of control, not the other person.
12. Others may provoke you to anger, but you do not have to respond angrily. When you respond as others want, they have the power to control you.
13. No one is the cause of you responding angrily. You have freedom of choice.
14. When you get mad, you are exercising your power, or you seek to avenge yourself.

15. You get some pleasure from hurting others, if you get angry repeatedly.
16. If you get angry often, you are unable to control your feelings.
17. Anger is a powerful emotion, either you control it, or you are controlled by it.

Draw a picture of your anger:

Often When We Are Angry, One Or More of These Are Going On:

1. We want something and are not getting it.
2. From past experience, we expect trouble.
3. We feel powerless to get what we want.

The principle of anger management techniques is for you to use your anger as a signal to *identify your problem/s and deal with it/them*; rather than act upon your anger by lashing out, and make the situation worse, or hold your angry feelings inside and let it become resentment.

Anger can lead to:

1. Angrily lashing out → to make the situation worse
2. Holding feelings inside→ creates resentment, physical symptoms

OR

You can identify the problem to handle or solve it. You do this by changing the thoughts you think. This is helpful when thinking about something that irritates you and makes you mad.

Can you think of someone or something that irritated you recently? *Write about it now:*

....

....

....

....

....

....

Have you ever felt any of the emotions below? How do they make you feel about yourself? *Go through the exercises below to be in better control of your emotions Write about when you felt the feelings below toward someone.*

• **Anger**: ....
....
....

• **Revenge**: ....
....
....

• **Jealousy**: ....
....
....

• **Resentment**: ....
....
....

How did you feel after you expressed the emotions above?

a. Did you feel happy, tired, or sad? *Write about your feelings, now.* ....
....
....

b. If you felt good, why? ....
....
....

c. Do you feel good when you hurt others?

....

....

d. How do you feel when others hurt you? ....

....

....

Write the words you use when talking with others about your anger.

....

....

....

For one week, monitor your inner self-talk and outer behavior. Write down your bodily reactions: breathing, clenched teeth, heavy breathing, tight neck or shoulder muscles, tight jaws, hot ears or other body parts, rigid, tense body posture, balled fist, rolled eyes.

....

....

....

....

....

....

....

....

....

....

Suggestions for Self Control and Self Discipline:

1. Learn to organize your immediate environment.

2. Put things back as you find them to help create order and stability for yourself.

3. Strive to be the same all the time

4. Learn to organize your life by keeping a daily list of things you plan to do – a *To Do List*. List your daily activities into A, B, C, D categories. 'A' represents activities with the highest priority.

5. Never settle for less than your best effort, best preparation, and best outcome, then your best follow-through.

6. Be your own coach, encourage yourself by saying and thinking positively.

7. Push yourself to be your best, and tell yourself you can.

8. Others may provoke you to anger, but you do not have to respond angrily.

9. When you do what others want, they are in control of you.

10. No one is the cause of you responding angrily. You have freedom of choice to behave and respond as you choose.

11. When you get mad, you are trying to protect your ego and self-pride.

12. If you get angry repeatedly, you get some pleasure from hurting others

13. If you get angry repeatedly, you are unable to control your feelings of frustration and have a need to "get even" to hurt as you feel you were hurt.

14. To keep your anger under control, do a kind act each day for yourself and another person.

15. Give yourself permission to be kind to yourself and others.

16. Find ways to be gentle, and kind to yourself and others

17. Breathe deeply often during the day to release tension and stress.

18. Work on being the same on both inside and outside yourself

19. Learn to meditate, (sit still, think on pleasant thought of nature) for one minutes, two times a day. Dr. Ida Greene lists the techniques in her book, *Light The Fire Within You*™

REAL ME – POST TEST ASSESSMENT

Circle the word(s) or number(s) that best fit you.

1. I would describe myself as a *nice | smart | angry | happy* person.

2. Others would describe me as a *nice | smart | angry | happy* person.

3. I get angry *1-5 | 5-10 | 10-20* times a day.

4. When I'm angry I *cry | scream | don't talk*.

5. This person makes me angry a lot *mom/dad | brother/sister | friend | teacher*.

6. They make me angry because they don't *listen to me | let me do what I want | care about me*.

7. When I get mad, they *ignore me | get mad at me | make me feel better*.

8. When I'm angry, I feel *better | worse | the same* than when I'm happy.

9. What makes me feel better when I'm angry is *talking about why I'm angry | playing/singing/dancing | ignoring the problem*.

10. I *do | don't* like myself when I'm angry.

HOW TO MANAGE YOUR ANGER

1. Anger does not have to be released like steam in a pressure cooker.

2. Venting/expressing your anger makes you feel better only for a moment, then regret, disappointment, and sorrow follow an emotional outburst.

3. The first step is to figure out what is causing you to get angry or react in an angry way.

    a. What are you saying to yourself inside your head?

    b. Do you feel taken advantage of, disrespected, ignored, used, not acknowledged?

    c. Do you have a fear of rejection?

    d. Do you like yourself?
    People who like themselves do not need to prove to someone else they are right.
    People who like themselves do not take or interpret things others say to them as a personal offense. They can give the other person the benefit of the doubt or let things pass without responding.

THE VALUE OF ANGER

Anger is a valuable signal, because it lets us know when something is wrong and needs to be corrected. The critical factor is whether your expression of anger is adding to the problem rather than solving the problem. You do not have a right to hurt others.

Often when we are angry, one or more of these things are going on:

1. We want something and are not getting it.
2. From past experience, we expect trouble.
3. We feel powerless to get what we want.

The principle of anger management techniques is for you to use your anger as a signal to *identify your problem/s and deal with it/them*; rather than act upon your anger by lashing out, and make the situation worse, or hold your angry feelings inside and let it become resentment.

ANGER CAN LEAD TO:

1. Angrily lashing out → to make the situation worse

2. Holding feelings inside → creates resentment, physical symptoms

OR

You can identify the problem to handle or solve it.

You do this by changing the thoughts you think. This is helpful when thinking about something that irritates you and makes you mad.

MYSELF

I have to live with myself, and so
I want to be fit for myself to know,
I want to be able, as days go by,
Always to look myself straight in the eye;
I don't want to stand, with the setting sun,
And hate myself for the things I've done.
I don't want to keep on a closet shelf,
a lot of secrets about myself.
And fool myself, as I come and go,
Into thinking that nobody else will know
The kind of person that I really am;
I don't want to dress up myself in a sham.
I want to go out with my head erect,
I want to deserve all men's respect;
But here in the struggle for fame and self,
I want to be able to like myself.
I don't want to look at myself and know
That I'm bluster and bluff and empty show,
I never can hide myself from me;
I see what others may never see;
I know what others may never know;
I never can fool myself, and so,
Whatever happens, I want to be
Self-respecting and conscience free.

— EDGAR A. GUEST

ANGER MANAGEMENT LOG

Name: ....Date:...........

Fill out this log each time you find yourself in an anger-provoking situation.

1. What was the situation? Who was involved?

    ....

    ....

2. On a scale of 1 to 5, how angry was I? Write a number to show how you felt
    • Irritated
    • Embarrassed
    • Upset
    • Mad
    • Very Mad

3. What did you say or do to respond? ....

    ....

    ....

4. Was your response appropriate? ..... or inappropriate?.....
    Why? ....

    ....

5. What was the consequence of my response? Did I get what I wanted? ....

Child (signature): ....

Staff/Guardian (signature) ....

WHAT IS AN ANGER WORKOUT?

A key point to remember is that your anger work-out, process is ongoing. We have to work out our frustration and anger; just we work out our body muscles. When you stop doing any of the work-outs, your old counterproductive anger habits are likely to reemerge. The more you work out, the less chance there is to be hurt by your old anger habits. Eventually, you will be able to do the work-outs on an automatic basis. When this happens you will be more productive in all aspects of your life. You will be: a more loving person, better: student, friend, associate, parent, more effective worker and live longer. Working out your anger shapes you up for live.

My prayer is that you live a long, stress free, fruitful life, and achieve all your goals and aspiration. Anger is neither good nor bad. It is just an emotion. When used wisely, it can allow you to be a powerful person, who is a pleasure to be around. I coach children, adults, entrepreneurs, and corporations on how to effectively communicate and negotiate to get what you desire.

You can reach me at:
> Tel.: 619-262-9951, or
> www.selfesteemcenter.org, or
> www.idagreene.com
> E-mail: idagreene@idagreene.com

We have several books to assist you, they are:
Anger Management Skills for Men
Anger Management Skills for Women
How to Improve Self-Esteem in Any Child
How to Improve Self-Esteem in the
  African American Child
Self-Esteem the Essence of You

Light the Fire Within You
Soft Power Negotiation Skills
Money – How to Get It, How to Keep It
How to be a Success in Business
Are You Ready for Success?
Say Goodbye to Your Smallness, Say Hello
    to Your Greatness
    and
Stirring Up the African American Spirit.

Now You Keep Track of
When Someone Made You Mad
and How You Responded